Bottom's Dream

A Play

Alan Poole

A SAMUEL FRENCH ACTING EDITION

FOUNDED 1830

SAMUELFRENCH.COM
SAMUELFRENCH-LONDON.CO.UK

FOR PRODUCTION ENQUIRIES

UNITED STATES AND CANADA

Info@SamuelFrench.com

1-866-598-8449

UNITED KINGDOM AND EUROPE

Theatre@SamuelFrench-London.co.uk

020-7255-4302

Each title is subject to availability from Samuel French, depending upon country of performance. Please be aware that BOTTOM'S DREAM may not be licensed by Samuel French in your territory. Professional and amateur producers should contact the nearest Samuel French office or licensing partner to verify availability.

MUSIC USE NOTE

Licensees are solely responsible for obtaining formal written permission from copyright owners to use copyrighted music in the performance of this play and are strongly cautioned to do so. If no such permission is obtained by the licensee, then the licensee must use only original music that the licensee owns and controls. Licensees are solely responsible and liable for all music clearances and shall indemnify the copyright owners of the play(s) and their licensing agent, Samuel French, against any costs, expenses, losses and liabilities arising from the use of music by licensees. Please contact the appropriate music licensing authority in your territory for the rights to any incidental music.

IMPORTANT BILLING AND CREDIT REQUIREMENTS

If you have obtained performance rights to this title, please refer to your licensing agreement for important billing and credit requirements.

CHARACTERS

Old Watch
Young Watch
Nick Bottom, a weaver
Ursula Bottom, his wife
Peter Quince, a carpenter
Robin Starveling, a tailor
Agnes Starveling, his wife
Francis Flute, a bellows-mender
Mrs Flute, his mother
Tom Snout, a tinker
Mrs Snout, his wife
Snug, a joiner
Alice Snug, his wife

Puck, a sprite
Peaseblossom
Cobweb
Moth } fairies
Mustardseed
Titania, Queen of the Fairies

The voices of—
Theseus, Duke of Athens
Hippolyta, Queen of the Amazons
Philostrate, Master of the Revels

SCENE

PROLOGUE and EPILOGUE   A Town at Midnight
BOTTOM'S DREAM   Athens, and a Wood Hard By

PRODUCTION NOTE

The play is designed for presentation on stage and in-the-round, with the action flowing from one area to the other. While this arrangement provides a very smooth transition from scene to scene, it is by no means essential and the action could be easily adapted to a conventional seating plan by use of the aisles and the immediate front-of-stage area. For this the use of rostra blocks would be helpful. In Act I, the Watch and Peter Quince would thus play before the curtain, and the artisans, after emerging from the house, would appear on stage for Scene 3, the same procedure being adopted by the wives in Scene 4. Act II would open on stage, with the women spying on their husbands from the aisles, where Puck would also appear. When the stage is emptied after the artisans scatter, their place would be taken by the wives to meet their returning husbands at the end of the scene. Scene 3 would be played before the curtain and the men's play in Scene 4 would be watched from the front of the side aisles by the ladies.

Scenic requirements are very simple: a bench or two for the meeting place, a log with perhaps a grassy bank or suspended bough for the palace wood and a suggestion of a classic portico against a cyclorama. A sequence of striking bells, different in pitch and pace and sounding in corridors adjacent to the auditorium, effectively locates the action of the dream between the first and last stroke of midnight. The door is a rather important item as it provides immediate identification of the characters and should be fitted with a hexagonal roller, preferably within the door's framework but above the door itself, upon which are the names, in sequence, of Quince, Starveling, Flute, Snout, Snug and Bottom.

The vertical bed is simple to construct, being an upright box shape, entered from behind in which Bottom and his wife stand with their heads against a raised headrest.

ACT I

PROLOGUE

Night. Clocks strike. The Watch, one old, one young, enter the arena carrying lanterns and staves

Old Watch (*in a quavering voice*)
    Twelve o'clock, look well to your lock,
    Your fire and your light,
    And so, good night!
Young Watch You should do better than that. No-one will ever hear you.
Old Watch (*testily*) Let be. Let be.
Young Watch (*lustily*) Twelve of the clock, a fine night and all's well!
Old Watch (*hissing*) Quiet, you young rip.
Young Watch What's up?
Old Watch You'll never make a good Watch that way. You'll wake everyone up.
Young Watch What do we call for, then?
Old Watch It's the custom, son. Besides, ne'er-do-wells will know we're about.
Young Watch (*apprehensively*) Are there any around these parts?
Old Watch You never can tell. They be stealthy ones.
Young Watch (*looking round apprehensively*) I don't think I like it much.
Old Watch That's why you don't shout too loud. You don't want to draw attention to yourself, see.
Young Watch But you said . . .
Old Watch (*irritably*) That's enough, younker. Hold quiet, hold quiet!
Young Watch Shall we get on then? We've a way to go.
Old Watch (*sitting down*) In good time. I allus sits here for a while.
Young Watch What for?
Old Watch You can see it all from here, the square, the church over there, the length of the street.
Young Watch But what does it matter?
Old Watch Sit here regular and you get respect, son. When the kine stand mist-deep on a June dawn and cats run home across the damp street; when yon steeple's black against a hard winter moon; when elm branches groan and tear in the November dark and when the Holy Child comes down in the Christmas bells, you learn, lad; you learn.
Young Watch What you on about?
Old Watch Just look down yon street—all them bedrooms full of people; the proud with their faces sagging like puddens; the milkmaid twitching her fingers in sleep round the teats; the scold hissing in her man's ear;

the old, shrinking under the covers with the stillness of death. Look! There's a light! See, it grows brighter; now it fades. Someone moving about—creased up with colic p'raps, or a mother giving the breast. Everything happens in those rooms, son. You drew your first breath there, and there, if you're lucky enough to escape yon crossroads gibbet, you'll give up your last.

Young Watch Shut up. You give me the horrors.

Old Watch And the dreams. The one that starts up and cries "Murder", and the warm young girl who sees her love riding down a moonbeam, and ...

Young Watch Don't you keep on!

Old Watch It's thoughts, lad. You've got to learn to live with your thoughts.

Young Watch Can we go now? I'm frozen stiff.

Old Watch (*getting up*) All right, all right. Let's leave 'em to their dreams.

They go off, their calls dying away on the night air

Old Watch (*as he goes*) Twelve o'clock, look well to your lock,
                               Your fire and your light,
                               And so, good night!

Young Watch Twelve of the clock, a fine night and all's well!

The CURTAINS *open on Nick Bottom and his wife in bed—nightcapped, presented vertically. Bottom snores deeply, regularly. Mrs Bottom stirs, wakes and groans*

Mrs Bottom Oh no, not again! How much more can I stand? Twenty-five years I've endured it! Every night for twenty-five years—Bottom in his pigswill sleep! (*Shouting*) Bottom!

Bottom stirs, champs, breathes quietly for a moment or two and then the deep rhythm starts again, rising quickly to a sonorous crescendo

I can't take any more; it's no use. I'm at breaking point; I'll be good for nothing in the morning unless I get some sleep. He'll be all right—the loom will be thumping in the shop like a thing alive and him whistling like a skylark. But my head! I can't bear to think of it! Bottom! Bottom, wake up!

There is a murmuring rumble from Bottom, nothing else

It isn't fair. I don't see why I should have to put up with it. I hate him, hate him! (*Her voice rises to a scream*) Bottom!

Bottom (*waking at last*) Mm? Y-yes, my love?

Mrs Bottom Pig!

Bottom Mm?

Mrs Bottom I said "Pig". Pig, pig, pig!

Bottom But, my dear ...

Mrs Bottom You're snoring again. Every night it's the same. You snoring pig!

Bottom You must be mistaken. I'm sure I ...

Mrs Bottom You stupid, stupid clown. I've got ears, haven't I? Sometimes I wish I hadn't!

Bottom I was just lying here dreaming quietly. (*He sighs*) A beautiful dream. It must have been the Watch who wakened you.

Mrs Bottom It wasn't the Watch, it was you, you braying donkey. The Watch has gone by already.

Bottom I didn't hear them.

Mrs Bottom Just shut up and listen, then.

Faintly, in the distance, the call of the Watch is heard

Now are you satisfied?

Bottom (*murmuring*) Midnight. The witching hour. I have an exposition of sleep come upon me. My dream; my beautiful dream. Something lovely, lovely beyond thought.

Mrs Bottom What are you talking about? I warn you I'll crack your pate with one of your own shuttles if you snore again.

Bottom (*almost asleep*) Bottom's dream—Peaseblossom, Cobweb, Mustard seed . . . My Lady!

The Lights fade to a Black-out, and—

the CURTAIN falls

SCENE 1

The portico of Theseus's Palace. It is night: a servant lights a hanging lamp; there are sounds of revelry

Peter Quince comes down through the audience into the arena

Quince (*to the audience*) I thought I'd find a goodly gathering here tonight. (*Rubbing his hands*) Wonderful times, aren't they? Our noble Duke and the fair Hippolyta soon to be married! Oh, everyone is very pleased—it's time he took a wife, you know. Of course, we didn't know what to expect when we heard he was returning from the wars with an Amazon bride! All those warlike women, fighting just like men! Well! But we needn't have worried; the Queen Hippolyta is a very lovely lady and she won all our hearts when she rode in procession through the city with our noble Duke. And now there's going to be celebrations and revelling and public holidays and all. I dare say there could be a chance for loyal citizens to get up some sort of entertainment for the Court—that has happened before. Now, there's a good idea! I wonder if I could persuade my friends, Bottom and Flute and Snout and the rest, to do something in that line? Bottom would jump at it but I'm not so sure of the others. Still, it's worth a try; I think I'll go and find them. (*To the audience*) Oh, I'd stay around, if I were you, and you'll almost certainly catch a glimpse of some of those important people up there at the palace. Perhaps even the Duke and his fair lady! See you later!

*Quince hurries off as the voices of Theseus and Hippolyta are heard,
coming through the music, talk and laughter*

Theseus (*off*)   Now, fair Hippolyta, our nuptial hour
Draws on apace: four happy days bring in
Another moon; but O! methinks how slow
This old moon wanes.

Hippolyta (*off*) Four days will quickly steep themselves in night;
Four nights will quickly dream away the time;
And then the moon, like to a silver bow
New-bent in heaven, shall behold the night
Of our solemnities.

Theseus (*off*)   Go, Philostrate,
Stir up the Athenian youth to merriments;
Awake the pert and nimble spirit of mirth;
Turn melancholy forth to funerals;
The pale companion is not for our pomp.
Hippolyta, I woo'd thee with my sword,
And won thy love doing thee injuries;
But I will wed thee in another key,
With pomp, with triumph, and with revelling.

The Lights on stage fade and the CURTAINS *close*

SCENE 2

A House—"Quince's Place". Evening

*Peter Quince emerges, smiles, rubs his hands, does a little skip, and goes on
his way. The door now shows it is "Starveling's Place". Robin Starveling
fomes out hurriedly with a pair of breeches and a jerkin flung after him,
collowed by his angry wife*

Mrs Starveling Go on then, and take these with you!

Starveling But what for?

Mrs Starveling Perhaps your good friends might like to help you out with
a stitch or two.

Starveling But it isn't often I go out and Peter Quince . . .

Mrs Starveling Peter Quince! It's all very well for him—he hasn't got a
wife and family to keep. Starveling by name and starveling by nature,
that's what it'll always be with you. Why did I marry a tailor?

*Mrs Starveling slams the door and Starveling goes ruefully on his way
through the arena*

The house now becomes "Flute's Place"

*The door opens gently and Flute tiptoes out, only to be arrested in his steps
by his mother's voice, breathy and wheezy*

Mrs Flute (*off*) Francis, Francis, is that you?

Flute (*miserably*) Yes, Mother?

Mrs Flute (*off*) Don't you go a step further till I come down.
Flute Oh dear. What shall I do? Shall I run for it? Better not, I suppose.

Mrs Flute enters, puffing, through the door

Mrs Flute Francis, you heard me. You're not going out.
Flute But I got to, Mum. All the other chaps is expecting me.
Mrs Flute Other chaps, indeed. Some girl or other, I'll be bound. Now who is she? (*She shakes him by the shoulder*)
Flute It isn't, Mum, honest. We've got a meeting, Quince and Bottom and Snug and the rest.
Mrs Flute I shall check up, mind, and the Lord keep you if I find you're not telling me the truth.
Flute It is true, Mum. I wouldn't have anything to do with girls. Much.
Mrs Flute There's a good boy now. You leave them nasty hussies alone. You'll be all right with your old mother.
Flute But I can't do for always, Mum. I'm getting a big lad now.
Mrs Flute So it is a girl! I knew it!
Flute No, no, no, Mum. It isn't! I told you it's Peter Quince and the others. (*Edging away*) I must go, Mum. I'll be late.

Flute runs off

Mrs Flute (*going indoors*) Oh dear, what a responsibility for a poor old widow woman! It's all getting too much for me.

Mrs Flute goes in

"Snout's Place" now shows on the door

Tom Snout comes out, followed by his smiling wife. He turns to her and gives her a kiss

Snout Good night, my love. I shan't be late.
Mrs Snout Never you mind, my darling. You have a good time with the lads.
Snout Don't wait up for me, now. Give us a kiss.
Mrs Snout Mm!

They kiss

Snout And kiss all the children for me, too.
Mrs Snout All right, all right. Go on with you now.
Snout Mary and Kathleen and Michael and Timmy and Susan and Deidre . . .
Mrs Snout Now, now, my love, will you be going. Yes, I'll kiss them—all fourteen.
Snout And tell 'em I love 'em all.
Mrs Snout I will that.
Snout And I love you too. Give us a kiss!
Mrs Snout Mm!

They kiss

Now go on with you.

Snout goes

Mrs Snout watches him go down the street, and when he reaches the corner she smiles and waves her apron

Snout (*calling back*) I love you, me darling.
Mrs Snout Get off! That's enough of your blarney, now.

Mrs Snout goes indoors

The door now shows "Snug's Place"

Snug and his wife come to the door

Mrs Snug Well, I think Peter Quince has taken leave of his senses.
Snug H-H-H-how do you m-m-m-mean?
Mrs Snug You in a play! Just listen to you.
Snug P-P-P-Peter knows b-b-best.
Mrs Snug You'll be the laughing stock of the town, or worse if you offend the Duke. Oh well, it's your funeral.

Mrs Snug goes in. Snug leaves

The house name now becomes "Bottom"

Nick Bottom comes out with exaggerated stealth, closes the door and moves away with tip-toe strides. The door opens again and Mrs Bottom comes out, folds her arms and looks down the street with a grim expression

Mrs Bottom All right, my boy. You don't fool me. Just wait till you come back home.

Mrs Bottom goes in, and the door closes behind her

Scene 3

A meeting place

Flute, the first of the artisans to arrive, creeps anxiously into the arena and sits. Snug, Snout and Starveling now join him and there is apprehensive talk and much head-shaking until Bottom arrives with a gay—"Now my brave lads!" Quince enters carrying rolled scripts which cascade from his arms, causing him agitation

Quince Is all our company here?
Bottom You were best to call them generally, man by man, according to the script.
Quince Here is the scroll of every man's name, which is thought fit, through all Athens, to play in our interlude before the Duke and Duchess on his wedding-day at night.
Bottom First, good Peter Quince, say what the play treats on; then read the names of the actors, and so grow to a point.
Quince Marry, our play is, "The most lamentable comedy, and most cruel death of Pyramus and Thisby".
Bottom A very good piece of work, I assure you, and a merry. Now, good

Peter Quince, call forth your actors by the scroll. Masters, spread yourselves.

Quince Answer as I call you. Nick Bottom, the weaver.

Bottom Ready. Name what part I am for, and proceed.

Quince You, Nick Bottom, are set down for Pyramus.

Bottom What is Pyramus? A lover, or a tyrant?

Quince A lover, that kills himself most gallantly for love.

Bottom That will ask some tears in the true performing of it: if I do it, let the audience look to their eyes; I will move storms, I will condole in some measure. To the rest: yet my chief humour is for a tyrant. I could play Ercles rarely, or a part to tear a cat in, to make all split.

The raging rocks
And shivering shocks
Shall break the locks
   Of prison gates:
And Phibbus' car
Shall shine from far
And make and mar
   The foolish Fates.

This was lofty! Now name the rest of the players. This is Ercles' vein, a tyrant's vein; a lover is more condoling.

Quince Francis Flute, the bellows-mender.

Flute Here, Peter Quince.

Quince You must take Thisby on you.

Flute What is Thisby? A wandering knight?

Quince It is the lady that Pyramus must love.

Flute Nay, faith, let me not play a woman; I have a beard coming.

Quince That's all one: you shall play it in a mask, and you may speak as small as you will.

Bottom An' I may hide my face, let me play Thisby too. I'll speak in a monstrous little voice, "Thisne, Thisne!" "Ah, Pyramus, my lover dear; thy Thisby dear, and lady dear!"

Quince No, no; you must play Pyramus; and Flute, you Thisby.

Bottom Well, proceed.

Quince Robin Starveling, the tailor.

Starveling Here, Peter Quince.

Quince Robin Starveling, you must play Thisby's mother. Tom Snout, the tinker.

Snout Here, Peter Quince.

Quince You, Pyramus's father; myself, Thisby's father; Snug, the joiner, you the lion's part; and, I hope, here is a play fitted.

Snug Have you the lion's part written? Pray you, if it be, give it to me, for I am slow of study.

Quince You may do it extempore, for it is nothing but roaring.

Bottom Let me play the lion too. I will roar, that I will do any man's heart good to hear me; I will roar, that I will make the Duke say, "Let him roar again, let him roar again".

Quince An you should do it too terribly, you would fright the Duchess and the ladies, that they would shriek; and that were enough to hang us all.

All That would hang us—every mother's son.

Bottom I grant you, friends, if that you should fright the ladies out of their wits, they would have no more discretion but to hang us; but I will aggravate my voice so that I will roar you as gently as any sucking dove; 1 will roar you as 'twere any nightingale.

Quince You can play no part but Pyramus; for Pyramus is a sweet-faced man; a proper man, as one shall see in a summer's day; a most lovely, gentlemanlike man; therefore, you must needs play Pyramus.

Bottom Well, I will undertake it. What beard were I best to play it in?

Quince Why, what you will. But masters, here are your parts; and I am to entreat you, request you, and desire you, to con them by tomorrow night, and meet me in the palace wood, a mile without the town, by moonlight: there will we rehearse; for if we meet in the city, we shall be dogged with company, and our devices known. In the meantime 1 will draw a bill of properties, such as our play wants. I pray you, fail me not.

Bottom We will meet; and there we may rehearse more obscenely and courageously. Take pains; be perfect; adieu.

Quince At the duke's oak we meet.

Bottom Enough; hold, or cut bow-strings.

SCENE 4

The Lights on the arena go down and up on the house which becomes Starveling's, Flute's, Snout's, Snug's and Bottom's, in quick succession as the women leave

Mrs Starveling Well if she hadn't called a meeting I would have done. It's time a stop was put to this.

Mrs Starveling goes off, grumbling

Mrs Flute (*wheezing and puffing*) I'm really too tired to go, but I'd better for Francis's sake. Oh dear, I hope he's not getting into bad company.

Mrs Snout (*smiling serenely*) Can't think what this is all about. Still it'll be nice to have a chat with the ladies and then back home to my Tom.

Mrs Snug Poor stuttering creature. 1 don't know how he'd get on without me. If those men are leading him astray they'll get plenty of words from me.

Mrs Bottom Nick Bottom needn't think he can ride roughshod over me! He's got a rude awakening just round the corner.

The Lights go down on the house and up on the arena

Mrs Starveling and Mrs Snug arrive at the meeting place together

Mrs Starveling Well, Alice, there's something very funny going on, if you ask me.

Mrs Snug I've got my suspicions.

Mrs Starveling Does Ursula Bottom know anything?

Mrs Snug What she doesn't she'll make up.

Mrs Starveling You can be sure of that.

Mrs Snug I'd never blame her husband, anyway, whatever he did.

Mrs Starveling Nor I. Must be a dog's life.

Mrs Snug Trouble is, he's leading our men astray.

Mrs Starveling Him and that Peter Quince.

Mrs Flute arrives all of a flutter

Mrs Flute Oh dear, thank goodness I'm not the last. I made sure I'd be late. It's me legs, you see.

Mrs Snug Here, sit down, Mrs Flute. Take the weight off your poor feet.

Mrs Flute They swells something terrible in the summer. I can't hardly get along.

Mrs Snug You poor thing. And now this worry. It's too bad.

Mrs Flute (*much agitated*) Oh Mrs Snug, what is it? I've been hearing such things.

Mrs Starveling That's what we're here to find out.

Mrs Snout enters wreathed in smiles

Mrs Snout Now, you lovely ladies. How nice to see you again!

Mrs Starveling Can't think what you have got to be so cheerful about.

Mrs Snout And why not, indeed?

Mrs Starveling You're in the same boat as the rest of us, you know. Your husband's running loose at nights.

Mrs Snout I don't know what you mean. He may go out with his friends once or twice but that is all.

Mrs Starveling But is that all? You wait till you hear what Mrs Bottom has to say. Look, here she comes.

Mrs Bottom enters

Mrs Bottom Now ladies. Are we all here?

Mrs Snug You're the last, Ursula.

Mrs Bottom Well let's get straight down to business. You all know why we've met?

Mrs Starveling (*grimly*) We do. We want to know what our men folk are up to.

Mrs Flute (*whimpering*) Oh dear; my poor little Francis.

Mrs Snout I don't know what you're worrying about. You can't want to deny our men a few simple pleasures.

Mrs Bottom But what pleasures? That's what we'd like to know.

Mrs Snout My Tom says they are just getting up a play.

Mrs Snug If you'll swallow that, you'll swallow anything. Snug in a play! I ask you!

Mrs Bottom The plain facts are that after living normal lives for years, Bottom, Snug, Snout, Starveling and . . .

Mrs Flute (*wailing*) Oh, not my Francis, too!

Mrs Bottom (*glaring at her*) The plain facts are that our men have taken
to going out secretly at nights, neglecting their wives and families.

Mrs Snout My Tom doesn't neglect me.

Mrs Starveling More's the pity.

Mrs Bottom We all have the evidence of our own eyes and ears. There's
Bottom mumbling over his pottage every supper time, and last night he
reared up in bed and called out "Thisby, Thisby, my love", all in his
sleep.

Mrs Snug I knew it! They're after the women.

Mrs Starveling Nick Bottom always had a roving eye. Not that anyone
would blame him, as Alice was saying just now.

Mrs Bottom And what may you mean by that, Agnes Starveling?

Mrs Starveling Well, he hasn't got much to keep him at home, has he?

Mrs Bottom How dare you! There's a warm house and a good table. I'd
be ashamed to own a man as skinny as yours.

Mrs Starveling And a tart tongue for afters, too.

Mrs Snout Now, ladies, now. Don't let's fall out.

Mrs Snug They're at a very funny age you know. And there are some girls
around this town'll run after anything in breeches.

Mrs Flute My Francis is only a boy. I hope he never thinks of things like
that.

Mrs Bottom Don't you believe it. Ask him what he was doing up Goose
Lane the other night.

Mrs Flute Goose Lane? Oh dear!

Mrs Bottom Yes, with that Jenny Golightly from the forge.

Mrs Flute (*tearfully*) And he gave me his word!

Mrs Bottom Men are all alike. None of 'em can be trusted. I want to know
who this Thisby is.

Mrs Snug There's no one of that name in these parts.

Mrs Bottom Just let me catch her, that's all. She'll soon feel the length of
my nails.

Mrs Starveling Well, you've certainly got problems, Ursula. I'm only
thankful my man isn't like that.

Mrs Bottom I shouldn't think he'd have the energy on what you feed him.

Mrs Starveling (*with assumed dignity*) Just because we don't all eat like
pigs at the trough it doesn't mean we're undernourished.

Mrs Bottom So that's the way of the wind. Pigs indeed! You forget, Agnes
Starveling, I've been in your kitchen, and I doubt if your Robin could
fancy anything out of there.

Mrs Starveling You vixen! Anyone could eat off the floor in my house, and
you know it.

Mrs Bottom Ay, could!

Mrs Snout Ladies, ladies!

Mrs Snug Well, none of us can afford to be complacent. We just don't
know what they're up to.

Mrs Flute Oh dear!

Mrs Snug Now take Snug . . .

Mrs Bottom No, you take him!

Mrs Snug Very funny. All right, I did take him—poor, witless creature when it comes to talking. He could hardly get out "I do" when Parson married us—we looked like being there till Martinmas.

Mrs Starveling I remember it well. We were all breathing on the words for him.

Mrs Snug But when it comes to cutting a mortice his hand's as steady and true as his heart.

Mrs Bottom (*acidly*) You've got off the point, Mrs Snug. Is he steady and true now?

Mrs Snug I don't know. I don't know. He's always played with the children of nights, made them toys out of little scraps of wood, and funny—he can always talk to them; the words come easy like fresh shavings from a plane.

Mrs Bottom The point, the point.

Mrs Snug Well, only yesterday our Mary came running in with tears streaming down her cheeks—her dad had frightened her, she said. Jumped out from behind his bench and roared at her like a lion, she said.

Mrs Starveling Poor little mite.

Mrs Snug Well, I gave him a piece of my mind at supper-time, I can tell you, and what do you think he said!

Mrs Starveling Go on!

Mrs Snug "I've got to practise to escape a hanging," he said.

Mrs Flute Oh terrible, terrible! What can be going on? It's the fairies, I know it is. Why can't they leave us alone? Our men, they've been pixilated.

Mrs Bottom I know what's bewitching them and it's not the fairies! Ladies, if we are going to keep our men the battle is on. We've everything to lose. Be vigilant, watch and follow! We shall meet again secretly, wherever our husbands meet, and then their devices shall be known. And now to our homes! Courage!

They all go off, talking

ACT II

SCENE 1

The curtains open on a woodland scene

A Fairy enters the arena on one side and Puck on the other, both proceeding towards the stage as they talk

Puck How now, spirit! whither wander you?

Fairy Over hill, over dale,
    Thorough bush, thorough brier,
  Over park, over pale,
    Thorough flood, thorough fire,
I do wander every where,
Swifter than the moon's sphere;
And I serve the fairy queen,
To dew her orbs upon the green:
The cowslips tall her pensioners be;
In their gold coats spots you see;
Those be rubies, fairy favours,
In those freckles like their savours:
I must go seek some dew-drops here,
And hang a pearl in every cowslip's ear.

Puck Away then be gone,
For my Fairy Master, Oberon,
A spell upon your Queen has cast,
To love the thing she sees at last
When on the world she opes her eye,
And spies that creature passing by.

Fairy Either I mistake your shape and making quite,
Or else you are that shrewd and knavish sprite
Call'd Robin Goodfellow: are you not he
That frights the maidens of the villagery;
Skim milk, and sometimes labour in the quern,
And bootless make the breathless housewife churn;
And sometime make the drink to bear no barm;
Mislead night-wanderers, laughing at their harm?
Those that Hobgoblin call you and sweet Puck,
You do their work, and they shall have good luck:
Are you not he?

Puck Fairy, thou speak'st aright;
I am that merry wanderer of the night.
I jest to Oberon, and make him smile

When I a fat and bean-fed horse beguile,
Neighing in likeness of a filly foal:
And sometime lurk I in a gossip's bowl,
In very likeness of a roasted crab;
And, when she drinks, against her lips I bob
And on her wither'd dewlap pour the ale.
The wisest aunt, telling the saddest tale,
Sometime for three-foot stool mistaketh me;
Then slip I from her bum, down topples she,
And "tailor" cries, and falls into a cough;
And then the whole quire hold their hips and loff;
And waxen in their mirth, and neeze, and swear
A merrier hour was never wasted there.
But now at once we must be gone,
For mortals to the wood are come,
And on this sward will gather soon
And talk beneath the fairy moon.

*Puck and the Fairy exit. Quince, Snug, Bottom, Flute, Snout and Starveling
enter and gather in the arena*

Bottom Are we all met?

Quince Pat, pat; and here's a marvellous convenient place for our re-
hearsal. This green plot shall be our stage, this hawthorn-brake our
tiring-house; and we will do it in action as we will do it before the Duke.

Bottom Peter Quince . . .

Quince What sayest thou, bully Bottom?

Bottom There are things in this comedy of Pyramus and Thisbe that will
never please. First, Pyramus must draw a sword to kill himself, which
the ladies cannot abide. How answer you that?

Snout By'r lakin, a parlous fear.

Starveling I believe we must leave the killing out, when all is done.

Bottom Not a whit: I have a device to make all well. Write me a prologue;
and let the prologue seem to say, we will do no harm with our swords,
and that Pyramus is not killed indeed; and for the more better assurance,
tell them that I, Pyramus, am not Pyramus, but Bottom the weaver: this
will put them out of fear.

Snout Will not the ladies be afeard of the lion?

Starveling I fear it, I promise you.

Bottom Master, you ought to consider with yourselves: to bring in—God
shield us!—a lion among ladies, is a most dreadful thing; for there is not
a more fearful wild-fowl than your lion living, and we ought to look to it.

Snout Therefore, another prologue must tell he is not a lion.

Bottom Nay, you must name his name, and half his face must be seen
through the lion's neck; and he himself must speak through, saying thus,
or to the same defect, "Ladies", or "Fair ladies", "I would wish you,"
or, "I would request you", or "I would entreat you, not to fear, not to
tremble: my life for yours. If you think I come hither as a lion, it were
pity of my life: no, I am no such thing: I am a man as other men are";

and there indeed let him name his name, and tell them plainly he is Snug
the joiner.
Quince Well, it shall be so. But there is two hard things, that is, to bring
the moonlight into a chamber; for, you know, Pyramus and Thisby meet
by moonlight.
Snug Doth the moon shine that night we play our play?
Bottom A calendar, a calendar! look in the almanack; find out moonshine,
find out moonshine.
Quince Yes, it doth shine that night.
Bottom Why, then may you leave a casement of the great chamber-
window, where we play, open; and the moon may shine in at the
casement.
Quince Ay; or else one must come in with a bush of thorns and a lanthorn,
and say he comes to disfigure, or to present, the person of Moonshine.
Then, there is another thing: we must have a wall in the great chamber;
for Pyramus and Thisby, says the story, did talk through the chink of a
wall.
Snug You can never bring in a wall. What say you, Bottom?
Bottom Some man or other must present Wall; and let him have some
plaster, or some rough-cast about him, to signify wall; and let him hold
his fingers thus, and through that cranny shall Pyramus and Thisby
whisper.
Quince If that may be, then all is well. Come, sit down, every mother's son,
and rehearse your parts.

They go up on stage and sit or walk about practising their lines in dumb show

The women creep into the arena

Mrs Snug There they are!
Mrs Flute Ssh!
Mrs Starveling But on their own. What are they up to?
Mrs Bottom Ah, this is their trysting place. You'll see.
Mrs Snug Let's hide, then, in these bushes and watch.
Mrs Snout I don't want to spy on my Tom.

They all round on her

Mrs Bottom If he's as innocent as you think, you've nothing to worry
about, have you?
Mrs Starveling No-one's any worse for being the wiser.
Mrs Snug It's just as well for them to know they can't trample us in the
mire.
Mrs Snout It still doesn't seem right, somehow.
Mrs Starveling Sh! Peter Quince is saying something.

The Women scatter and hide to listen

Quince Now, Pyramus, you begin. When you have spoken your speech,
enter into that brake, and so everyone according to his cue.
Snug W-W-What's "cue"?

Quince That is when you have to speak; you take your cue from the actor
  before you.
Snug (*puzzled*) Oh.
Quince Look you here. (*He goes in among them to explain with the aid of
  his script*)

Puck appears

Puck What hempen homespuns have we swaggering here,
   So near the cradle of the Fairy Queen?
   What, a play toward? I'll be an auditor;
   An actor too perhaps, if I see cause.
Quince Speak, Pyramus! Thisby, stand forth!
Bottom (*as Pyramus*) Thisby, the flowers of odious savours sweet . . .
Quince Odours—odours!
Bottom (*as Pyramus*)   . . . odours savours sweet;
   So hath thy breath, my dearest Thisby dear.
   But hark, a voice! Stay thou but here awhile,
   And by and by I will to thee appear.

Bottom exits

Puck   A stranger Pyramus than e'er played here,
                         Ass, to our Fairy Queen he shall appear!

Puck exits

Flute Must I speak now?
Quince Ay, for you must understand he goes but to see a noise he heard
  and is to come again.
Flute (*as Thisby*) Most radiant Pyramus, most lily-white of hue,
   Of colour like the red rose on triumphant brier,
   Most brisky juvenal and eke most lovely Jew,
   As true as truest horse that yet would never tire,
   I'll meet thee, Pyramus, at Ninny's tomb . . .
Quince "Ninus' tomb", man! Why you must not speak that yet. That you
  answer to Pyramus. You speak all your parts at once, cues and all.
  Pyramus enter—your cue is past. It is "never tire".
Others (*echoing and peering off*) Pyramus!
Mrs Starveling I do believe it is a play.
Mrs Bottom Nonsense. They're up to no good. Just you wait.
Mrs Snout My Tom wouldn't lie to me, that I know.
Quince Give him the cue again.
Flute (*as Thisby*) As true as truest horse that yet would never tire.

Bottom enters wearing an ass's head, followed by Puck

Bottom (*as Pyramus*) If I were fair, Thisby, I were only thine . . .
Quince O monstrous! O strange! We are haunted!
       Pray masters! Fly masters! Help!

The men all run off, leaving Bottom and Puck

Puck I'll follow you; I'll lead you about a round,
 Through bog, through bush, through brake, through brier.
 Sometime a horse I'll be, sometime a hound,
 A hog, a headless bear, sometime a fire;
 And neigh, and bark, and grunt, and roar, and burn,
 Like horse, hound, hog, bear, fire, at every turn.

Puck exits

Bottom Why do they run away? This is knavery to make me afeard.

Snout enters

Snout O Bottom, thou art changed. What do I see on thee?
Bottom What do you see? You see an ass-head of your own, do you?

Snout exits. Quince enters

Quince Bless thee, Bottom, bless thee! Thou art translated.

Quince exits

Bottom I see their knavery. This is to make an ass of me, to fright me if they
 could; but I will not stir from this place, do what they can. I will walk up
 and down here, and will sing that they shall hear I am not afraid.
 The ousel-cock, so black of hue,
 With orange-tawny bill,
 The throstle with his note so true,
 The wren with little quill . . .

Bottom stumps off, singing

The Women come forward rather sheepishly

Mrs Snug Well, what do you make of that?
Mrs Starveling Passing strange. Methinks we are the fools, after all.
Mrs Snug So it is a play they're doing.
Mrs Snout I told you that, but you wouldn't listen. It's for the Duke's
 wedding.
Mrs Flute Oh, what a relief!
Mrs Bottom All right, all right! You're very easily satisfied, aren't you? I
 suppose I'm to blame for it all.
Mrs Starveling Now come, Ursula. We've all said hard things. Let by-
 gones by bygones.
Mrs Snug Yes, we can all be glad we were wrong.
Mrs Bottom Weak as water, that's what you are! I'll never humble myself
 before any man! Bottom's got a lot to answer for.
Mrs Snug Look, here come the men.

*The Artisans, with the exception of Bottom, come through the audience
into the arena*

The two groups stand in embarrassed silence for a moment

Quince (*with a little laugh*) Eh, did you see?

Mrs Bottom (*tartly*) We did.
Mrs Starveling (*impulsively*) Oh, Robin, I didn't trust you! (*She goes across to Starveling*)
Tom Snout (*going across to his wife*) I know my little girl wouldn't think that.
Mrs Snout Oh no, Tom.
Snout Give us a kiss then.

Snout and Mrs Snout kiss

Flute (*going to his mother*) I told you it was all right, Mother.
Mrs Snug (*crossing*) Come here, Snug, lad. Now don't try to say anything. Let's go home to the children.

Mrs Snug links her arm in Snug's, and they start to move off, followed by the others, except for Mrs Bottom

Mrs Bottom (*left behind*) Just a minute. What about Bottom?

They all turn and look at her

Quince We know nothing, Ursula. He's vanished.
Mrs Bottom He can't just disappear. He must be somewhere in the wood. You'll have to find him.
Quince We've been chased and belaboured in those coverts. We can't go back there again.
Mrs Bottom But you can't just leave him.
Starveling I'm sorry there's nothing we can do.
Snout Perhaps he's gone home another way.

They move off

Mrs Bottom Wait a minute. You can't go like this! Please listen! Please!

They all leave

Mrs Bottom is alone, and anxious now

They've all got their men back but me. Trust Bottom. (*She goes up on stage and calls*) Bottom! Just you come out of there at once! Do you hear me? Bottom! Bottom, you'll regret this! I know you're there! (*Tearfully*) Nicholas, won't you come back to me? Please, Nick. I'll be different in the future, I promise. Oh dear; oh dear!

Mrs Bottom leaves, weeping

A faint braying is heard in the distance

SCENE 2

The same

Bottom enters on stage, still singing

Bottom The ousel-cock, so black of hue,
      With orange-tawny bill,
      The throstle with his note so true,
      The wren with the little quill.

He marches up and down. There is faery music

  Titania enters

Titania What angel wakes me from my flow'ry bed?

Bottom (*continuing*)
      The finch, the sparrow, and the lark,
      The plain-song cuckoo gray,
      Whose note full many a man doth mark,
      And dares not answer, nay;

Titania (*coming down to him*)
    I pray thee, gentle mortal, sing again;
    Mine ear is much enamour'd of thy note;
    So is mine eye enthralled to thy shape;
    And thy fair virtue's force, perforce, doth move me,
    On the first view, to say, to swear, I love thee.

Bottom (*sitting down*) Methinks, mistress, you should have little reason for that: and yet, to say the truth, reason and love keep little company together now-a-days. The more the pity, that some honest neighbours will not make them friends.

Titania Thou art wise as thou art beautiful.

Bottom Not so, neither; but if I had wit enough to get out of this wood, I have enough to serve mine own turn.

Titania (*to quiet music*)
    Out of this wood do not desire to go:
    Thou shalt remain here, whe'r thou wilt or no.
    I am a spirit of no common rate;
    The summer still doth tend upon my state;
    And I do love thee: therefore, go with me;
    I'll give thee fairies to attend on thee,
    And they shall fetch thee jewels from the deep,
    And sing, while thou on pressed flowers dost sleep:
    And I will purge thy mortal grossness so
    That thou shalt like an airy spirit go.
    Peaseblossom! Cobweb! Moth! and Mustardseed!

Four Fairies—Peaseblossom, Cobweb, Moth and Mustardseed—enter

Peaseblossom Ready.

Cobweb And I.

Moth And I.

Mustardseed And I.

All Four Where shall we go?

Titania (*to quiet music*)
> Be kind and courteous to this gentleman;
> Hop in his walks, and gambol in his eyes;
> Feed him with apricocks and dewberries,
> With purple grapes, green figs, and mulberries,
> The honey-bags steal from the humble-bees,
> And for night-tapers crop their waxen thighs,
> And light them at the fiery glow-worm's eyes,
> To have my love to bed, and to arise;
> And pluck the wings from painted butterflies
> To fan the moonbeams from his sleeping eyes;
> Nod to him, elves, and do him courtesies.

Peaseblossom Hail, mortal!

Cobweb Hail!

Moth Hail!

Mustardseed Hail!

Bottom I cry your worship's mercy, heartily: I beseech your worship's name.

Cobweb Cobweb.

Bottom I shall desire you of more acquaintance, good Master Cobweb: if I cut my finger, I shall make bold with you. Your name, honest gentleman?

Peaseblossom Peaseblossom.

Bottom I pray you, commend me to Mistress Squash, your mother, and to Master Peascod, your father. Good Master Peaseblossom, I shall desire you of more acquaintance too. Your name, I beseech you, sir?

Mustardseed Mustardseed.

Bottom Good Master Mustardseed, I know your patience well: that same cowardly, giant-like ox-beef hath devoured many a gentleman of your house. I promise you, your kindred hath made my eyes water ere now. I desire you of more acquaintance, good Master Mustardseed.

Titania (*to quiet music*)
> Come, wait upon him; lead him to my bower.
> The moon methinks, looks with a watery eye;
> And when she weeps, weeps every little flower,
> Lamenting some enforced chastity.

Bottom brays and the Fairies cover their ears

> Tie up my love's tongue, bring him silently.

They all exit, as—

the CURTAINS *close*

A meeting place

Quince, Flute, Snout and Starveling enter the arena

Quince Have you sent to Bottom's house? Is he come home yet?
Starveling He cannot be heard of. Out of doubt he is transported.
Flute If he come not, then the play is marred: it goes not forward, doth it?
Quince It is not possible: you have not a man in all Athens able to discharge Pyramus but he.
Flute No; he hath simply the best wit of any handicraft man in Athens.
Quince Yea, and the best person too; and he is a very paramour for a sweet voice.
Flute You must say, "paragon": a paramour is, God bless us! a thing of naught.

Snug enters

Snug Masters, the Duke is coming from the temple, and there is two or three lords and ladies more married: if our sport had gone forward, we had all been made men.
Flute O sweet bully Bottom! Thus hath he lost sixpence a day during his life: He could not have 'scaped sixpence a day: an the Duke had not given him sixpence a day for playing Pyramus, I'll be hanged; he would have deserved it: sixpence a day in Pyramus, or nothing.

Bottom enters

Bottom Where are these lads? Where are these hearts?

The others are overjoyed

Quince Bottom! O most courageous day! A most happy hour!
Bottom Masters, I am to discourse wonders: but ask me not what; for if I tell you, I am no true Athenian. I will tell you everything, right as it fell out.
Quince Let us hear, sweet Bottom.
Bottom Not a word of me. All that I will tell you is, that the Duke hath dined. Get your apparel together, good strings to your beards, new ribbons to your pumps; meet presently at the palace; every man look o'er his part; for the short and the long is, our play is preferred. In any case, let Thisby have clean linen; and let not him that plays the lion pare his nails, for they shall hang out for the lion's claws. And, most dear actors eat no onions nor garlic, for we are to utter sweet breath, and I do not doubt but to hear them say, it is a sweet comedy. No more words; away, go!

They all exit

SCENE 4

Theseus's Palace. Night

The voice of Theseus is heard, through music

Theseus   Come, now; what masques, what dances shall we have,
             To wear away this long age of three hours
             Between our after supper and bedtime?
             Where is our usual manager of mirth?
             What revels are in hand? Is there no play,
             To ease the anguish of a torturing hour?
             Call Philostrate.
Philostrate   Among other sports,
             A play there is, my lord, some ten words long,
             Which is as brief as I have known a play;
             But by ten words, my lord, it is too long,
             Which makes it tedious; for in all the play
             There is not one word apt, one player fitted.
Theseus   What are they that do play it?
Philostrate Hard-handed men that work in Athens here,
             Which never laboured in their minds till now,
             And now have toiled their unbreathed memories
             With this same play against your nuptial.
Theseus   And we will hear it.
Philostrate   No, my noble lord;
             It is not for you: I have heard it over,
             And it is nothing, nothing in the world.
Theseus   I will hear that play;
             For never anything can be amiss,
             When simpleness and duty tender it.
             Go, bring them in; and take your places, ladies.

*Mrs Bottom, Mrs Snug, Mrs Snout, Mrs Flute and Mrs Starveling enter
and occupy low stools in the arena*

Mrs Starveling Just fancy, the likes of us being invited to the Duke's
   festivities!
Mrs Bottom Oh they're real gentry, you can tell that.
Mrs Snug You would know, of course.
Mrs Bottom That Master of the Revels, what's his name—Philostrate! He
   sent his servant for me, he did. Come knocking on my door to summon
   me to the Palace!
Mrs Starveling Can't think why they picked on you.
Mrs Snug Yes, what was wrong with the rest of us?
Mrs Snout Now, ladies, we're here, that's all that matters. Someone had
   to be asked.

Mrs Bottom Well, into this room I goes and there he sits behind this big desk.

Mrs Flute Who? The Duke?

Mrs Bottom No, stupid! That Philostrate. "Mistress Bottom", he said, all haughty—like up in his nose—I could've laughed!—"Mistress Bottom", he said, "In case your husband's play is preferred the Duke will be graciously pleased for you and your friends to be received at the Palace."

Mrs Snout And here we are!

There is music while the Court assembles. The women comment on the imaginary scene

Mrs Starveling Oh, look! They're coming.

They all look up the arena

Mrs Snug That'll be the Queen Hippolyta on our noble Duke's arm.

Mrs Snout Oh, isn't she lovely!

They curtsy and smile as the imaginary couple passes through

Mrs Starveling (*her eyes following*) Just look at that dress! I could just see myself in a dress like that.

Mrs Bottom (*looking up the arena*) There's the Lady Hermia with her father, Old Egeus, and Lysander.

They curtsy again

They say there was trouble there, you know.

Mrs Starveling What sort of trouble?

Mrs Bottom He wanted her to marry that there Demetrius. You know him that was going around with Nedar's daughter, Helena, before he gave her the chuck.

Mrs Snug Look, look! There's Helena now.

Mrs Snout And Demetrius with her. Don't they make a lovely couple!

They curtsy as the two imaginary courtiers pass

Mrs Starveling (*slyly*) Seems you were wrong about that, Ursula.

Mrs Snug (*playing up*) You must have been misinformed in your court circles.

Mrs Bottom Ah, but they're together again now, and Egeus has given his blessing to Lysander and Hermia.

Mrs Snug Listen, listen! What's that?

There is the sound of a drum and into the arena march the Artisans, led by Peter Quince

The Women laugh and clap heartily

Mrs Bottom Give us the play, Nicholas.

Mrs Snug Yes, do your best, Snug, lad.

Mrs Snout (*laughing*) Just look at my Tom. What's he got on?

The Artisans mount the stage and line up sheepishly. Peter Quince comes forward and bows. The Women clap again

Quince (*as Prologue*)

Gentles, perchance you wonder at this show;
But wonder on, till truth makes all things plain.
This man is Pyramus, if you would know;
This beauteous lady Thisbe is, certain.
This man with lime and rough-cast, doth present
Wall, that vile wall which did these lovers sunder;
And through this wall's chink, poor souls, they are content
To whisper, at the which let no man wonder.
This man, with lanthorn, dog, and bush of thorn,
Presenteth Moonshine; for, if you will know
By moonshine did these lovers think no scorn
To meet at Ninus' tomb, there to woo.
This grisly beast which Lion hight by name,
The trusty Thisbe coming first by night,
Did scare away, or rather did affright;
And as she fled, her mantle she did fall,
Which Lion vile with bloody mouth did stain.
Anon comes Pyramus, sweet youth and tall,
And finds his trusty Thisbe's mantle slain:
Whereat, with blade, with bloody blameful blade,
He bravely broached his boiling bloody breast;
And Thisbe tarrying in mulberry shade,
His dagger drew and died. For all the rest,
Let Lion, Moonshine, Wall and lovers twain,
At large discourse while here they do remain.

All the Artisans exit, except Snout

Snout (*as a wall*)

In this same interlude it doth befall
That I—one Snout by name—present a wall.
And such a wall as I would have you think,
That had in it a crannied hole or chink,
Through which the lovers, Pyramus and Thisbe,
Did whisper often very secretly.
This loam, this roughcast and this stone doth show
That I am that same wall: the truth is so.
And this the cranny is, right and sinister,
Through which the fearful lovers are to whisper.

He holds up his fingers

Mrs Snout (*clapping*) Well spoken, Wall!
Others Sh!

Mrs Snout retires in confusion

Bottom, as Pyramus, enters and approaches the Wall

Pyramus O grim-looked night! O night with hue so black!
O night which ever art when day is not!
O night! O night! alack, alack, alack!
I fear my Thisbe's promise is forgot.
And thou, O wall, O sweet, O lovely wall!
Show me thy chink to blink through with mine eyne.

Wall holds up his fingers

Thanks, courteous Wall: Jove shield thee well for this!
But what see I? No Thisbe do I see.
O wicked wall! through whom I see no bliss;
Cursed be thy stones for thus deceiving me!

He takes a kick at Wall, and the Women laugh

Mrs Snout (*shaking her fist*) Don't you dare kick my Tom!
Mrs Starveling Methinks the wall should curse him back.
Pyramus (*to the audience*) No, in truth, he should not. "Deceiving me" is
Thisbe's cue: she is to enter now, and I am to spy her through the wall.
You shall see, it will fall pat as I told you. Yonder she comes.

Flute, as Thisbe, enters and approaches the Wall

Thisbe O wall! full often hast thou heard my moans,
For parting my fair Pyramus and me:
My cherry lips have often kissed thy stones,
Thy stones with lime and hair knit up in thee.
Pyramus I see a voice: now will I to the chink,
To spy an I can hear my Thisbe's face.
Thisbe!
Thisbe My love! thou art my love, I think.
Pyramus Think what thou wilt, I am thy lover's grace;
O kiss me through the hole of this vile wall!

They try to kiss

Thisbe I kiss the wall's hole, not your lips at all!
Pyramus Wilt thou at Ninny's tomb meet me straightway?
Thisbe 'Tide life, 'tide death, I come without delay.

Pyramus and Thisbe leave in opposite directions

Wall Thus have I, Wall, my part discharged so;
And being done, this Wall away doth go.

Wall leaves

*The Women laugh and clap, and then the voices of Hippolyta and Theseus
are heard*

Hippolyta This, my Lord, is the silliest stuff that ever I heard.
Theseus The best in this kind, Hippolyta, are but shadows: and the worst
are no worse if imagination mend them.

*Snug enters as Lion, and Starveling as Moonshine, carrying bush, lantern
and dog*

Lion You, ladies, you whose gentle hearts do fear
The smallest monstrous mouse that creeps on floor,
May now, perchance, both quake and tremble here,
When lion rough in wildest rage do roar.
Then know that I as Snug the joiner am
For if I should as Lion come in strife
Into this place 'twere pity on my life.

He bows and the Women clap

Mrs Snug Did you hear that? I just can't believe it! That was my Snug!
Moonshine This lanthorn doth the horned moon present ...
Mrs Bottom You're right there, Robin Starveling, you bag of bones!
Mrs Starveling Look here, Ursula, I've just about had enough of your
insults.
Moonshine (*patiently, doggedly*)
This lanthorn doth the horned moon present,
Myself the man i' the moon do seem to be.
Mrs Bottom You the man in the moon! That's a laugh! You're so thin
you'd fall out!
Starveling (*as himself, and now angrily*) All I have to tell you is that the
lanthorn is the moon, I the man i' the moon, this thorn bush my thorn
bush, and this dog my dog.

Thisbe enters

Thisbe This is old Ninny's tomb. Where is my love?

Lion jumps out at Thisbe

With a shriek, Thisbe runs off

Lion savages her mantle. The Women show their pleasure

Mrs Snug Well roared, Lion!
Mrs Flute Well run, Thisbe!
Mrs Starveling Well shone, Moon!

Pyramus enters

Pyramus Sweet moon, I thank thee for thy sunny beams;
I thank thee, moon for shining now so bright;
For by thy gracious, golden, glittering gleams,
I trust to taste of truest Thisbe's sight.
But stay, O spite!
But mark, poor knight,
What dreadful dole is here!
Eyes do you see?
How can it be?
O dainty duck! O dear!
Thy mantle good,

What! stained with blood!
Approach ye Furies fell!
O Fates, come come,
Cut thread and thrum;
Quail, crush, conclude and quell!

He falls on his knees

O! wherefore, Nature, didst thou lions frame?
Since lion vile hath here deflowered my dear?
Which is—no, no!—which was—the fairest dame
That lived, that loved, that liked, that looked with cheer. (*Rising*)
Come tears confound;
Out sword and wound
The pap of Pyramus:
Ay, that left pap,
Where heart doth hop:
Thus die I, thus, thus, thus.

He stabs himself and falls

Now am I dead,
Now am I fled;
My soul is in the sky:
Tongue, lose thy light!
Moon, take thy flight!
Now, die, die, die, die, die.

He dies. The Women clap and laugh. Bottom sits up and gestures angrily to them to be quiet

Mrs Snout Look, here comes Thisbe, again.
Thisbe Asleep, my love?
What, dead, my love?
O Pyramus arise!
Speak, speak! Quite dumb?
Dead, dead? A tomb
Must cover thy sweet eyes.
These lily lips,
This cherry nose,
These yellow cowslip cheeks,
Are gone, are gone.
Lovers make moan—
His eyes were green as leeks!
Tongue, not a word!
Come, trusty sword,
Come blade my breast imbrue!
And farewell, friends.
Thus Thisby ends,
Adieu, adieu, adieu.

Thisbe stabs herself and falls

Bottom and Flute rise

Snug, Snout and Starveling enter

All bow to the clapping of the audience. The actors, with the exception of Bottom, come down into the arena and join the women. Together they move off through the audience, talking as they go

Mrs Starveling (*with her husband*) Oh, Robin, that was lovely!
Mrs Flute (*with her son*) You're a good boy, Francis.
Mrs Snug (*with her husband*) Where's the stutter gone, lad?
Snug I, I, I . . .
Mrs Snug All right, all right.
Snout How about that, my love?
Mrs Snout Oh, Tom! You were wonderful! I was so proud!
Snout Give us a kiss, then, me darling.
Mrs Snout Mm!

Snout and Mrs Snout kiss

All exit except Bottom and Mrs Bottom

Mrs Bottom (*alone, and now very subdued*) Nicholas, I've been a wicked woman. Oh, Nick, I'm sorry! I'll be kind in the future.

Bottom appears to ponder, and then, with a generous smile, turns to her and holds out his arms. Mrs Bottom goes up on stage and the CURTAINS *close on their reconciliation. The arena lights go down and in the darkness the voice of Theseus is heard*

Theseus The iron tongue of midnight hath told twelve;
    Lovers, to bed; 'tis almost fairy time.
    I fear we shall outsleep the coming morn,
    As much as we this night have overwatched.
    This palpable gross play hath well beguiled
    The heavy gait of night. Sweet friends, to bed.
    A fortnight hold we this solemnity,
    In nightly revels and new jollity.

EPILOGUE

The Bottoms in bed. Nightcapped

Bottom (*waking*) I've had a most rare vision. I have had a dream, past the
wit of man to say what dream it was: man is but an ass, if he go about
to expound this dream. Methought I was—there is no man can tell what.
Methought I was—and methought I had—but man is but a patched fool
if he will offer to say what methought I had. The eye of man hath not
heard, the ear of man hath not seen, man's hand is not able to taste, his
tongue to conceive, nor his heart to report, what my dream was. I will
get Peter Quince to write a ballad of this dream: it shall be called
Bottom's Dream, because it hath no bottom.

Mrs Bottom (*waking*) Now what is it? Are we to get no peace tonight? If
you're not snoring, you're talking. What's the matter with you?

Bottom (*groaning*) My dream, my beautiful dream! All night long it's been
with me.

Mrs Bottom All night long? What are you babbling about? It's only
midnight.

Bottom (*puzzled*) Midnight? But . . .

Mrs Bottom Yes, midnight. Minutes ago you woke me with your snoring
and now you're talking your stupid head off.

Bottom Ursula, my dear, you said you'd be kind . . .

Mrs Bottom (*acidly*) Kind? To you? You must have been dreaming.

The Watch is heard in the distance

Now do you believe me? There's the Watch coming back down the
street.

The Old Watch enters, followed by the Young Watch

Old Watch Twelve o'clock, look well to your lock,
  Your fire and your light,
  And so good night!

Young Watch Twelve of the clock, a fine night and all's well!

*They sit and rest, and now there is faery music through which we hear Titania's
voice. The stage lights are dimmed*

Titania Sleep thou, and I will wind thee in my arms.
  Fairies, be gone, and be all ways away.
  So doth the woodbine the sweet honeysuckle
  Gently entwist; the female ivy so
  Enrings the barky fingers of the elm.
  O, how I love thee! How I dote on thee!

Bottom (*crying out*) Where have I been? Let me dream again!

The CURTAINS close; a single light is left on the arena

Young Watch It's a long night.

Old Watch That's the job, son. Patience. You'll get used. Give it time.

Young Watch It's all time—and waiting.

Old Watch When midnight's gone, you'll find, and you're in the climbing hours; when the flittermouse flackers through the rafters to its hanging place, then it won't be long to the clearing of throats, the cursing of hardened boots, steaming morning gruel and gummy eyes blinking at the dawn.

Young Watch Mine are dropping already and the night only half gone.

Old Watch (*rising*) Come on, lad. All's quiet. I'll show you sweet hay for an hour.

The Old and Young Watch leave, each giving his cry

As their voices die away, leaving the arena in darkness, the clocks state the remaining notes of this midsummer midnight

FURNITURE AND PROPERTY LIST

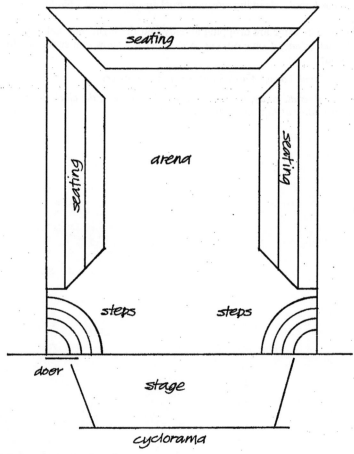

See also Production Note

Vertical bed
Benches
Stools
Log
Grassy bank
Classical portico cut-out
Door with differing name signs

2 lanterns (**Watch**)
2 staves (**Watch**)
Roll of scripts (**Quince**)
Ass's head (**Bottom**)
Lantern, dog, bush of thorn (**Starveling/Moon**)
Lime, rough-cast (**Snout/Wall**)
Sword (**Bottom/Pyramus**)
Lion mask (**Snug/Lion**)
Bloodstained mantle (**Flute/Thisby**)

LIGHTING PLOT

Property fittings required: hanging lamp
Various settings on open stage

ACT I. Night

To open: Spot on **Watch**

Cue 1	As CURTAINS open *Bring up spots on vertical bed*	(Page 2)
Cue 2	**Bottom:** "My Lady!" *Fade to Black-out, then up on* **Theseus's** *palace*	(Page 3)
Cue 3	**Theseus:** ". . . and with revelling." *Cross-fade to front lighting*	(Page 4)
Cue 4	**Mrs Bottom** closes door *Cross-fade to* **Quince's** *house*	(Page 6)
Cue 5	**Bottom:** ". . . hold, or cut bowstrings." *Cross-fade to front lighting*	(Page 8)
Cue 6	**Mrs Bottom:** ". . . just round the corner." *Cross-fade to arena lighting*	(Page 8)

ACT II. Night

To open: Bring up lighting on Woodland scene

Cue 7	**Bottom:** "The wren with the little quill." *Change of lighting for Faery scene*	(Page 18)
Cue 8	**Fairies** and **Bottom** exit *Cross-fade to* **Quince's** *house*	(Page 19)
Cue 9	**Bottom:** "No more words; away, go!" *Cross-fade to* **Theseus's** *palace*	(Page 20)
Cue 10	CURTAINS close on **Bottom** and **Mrs Bottom** *Fade to Black-out*	(Page 27)
Cue 11	At start of Epilogue *Spot on* **Bottom** *and* **Mrs Bottom** *in bed, faint light to cover entrance of* **Watch**	(Page 28)
Cue 12	**Bottom** and **Mrs Bottom** sink to rest *Dim all lighting*	(Page 28)
Cue 13	**Bottom:** "Let me dream again!" *Fade to single light on arena*	(Page 28)
Cue 14	The **Watch** exit *Fade to Black-out*	(Page 29)

EFFECTS PLOT

ACT I

Lightning Source UK Ltd.
Milton Keynes UK
UKHW02f2101230318
319956UK00005B/250/P